SWIMMING

BY NATE LeBOUTILLIER

CREATIVE ✷ EDUCATION

CONTENTS

INTRODUCTION

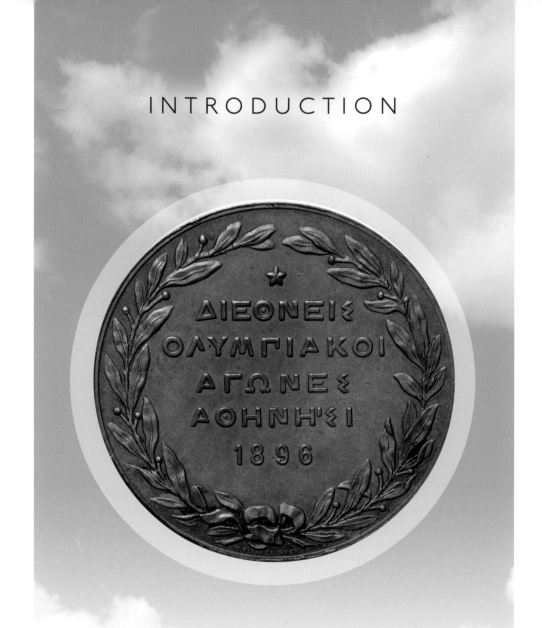

Throughout human history, people have always sought to challenge themselves, to compete against others, and to discover the limits of their capabilities. Such desires can turn destructive, leading to war. But the ancient Greeks also recognized the good in these human traits, and it was because of them that the Olympic Games—featuring running races, jumping contests, throwing competitions, and wrestling and boxing matches—began more than 2,700 years ago. The ancient Olympics ended in A.D. 393, but the Games were revived in 1896 in hopes of promoting world peace through sports. Fittingly, the first "modern" Olympics were held in Athens, Greece, but they moved around the world every four years after that. In 2009, it was announced that the Games would be held in South America for the first time, going to Rio de Janeiro, Brazil, in 2016.

Every 1896 Olympian received a medal reading "International Olympic Games, Athens 1896"

Only five sports have been contested at every Summer Olympic Games: athletics (known today as track and field), cycling, fencing, gymnastics, and swimming. In the first three Olympics, swimming competitions were held not in pools but in open water. These sites included the Mediterranean Sea in Athens, Greece, in 1896; the Seine River in Paris, France, in 1900; and an artificial lake in Forest Park, near St. Louis, Missouri, in 1904. In 1908 in London, England, Olympic swimming was permanently moved to a pool—in that case, one built inside the Games' outdoor track and field oval.

Early stars of Olympic swimming included Duke Kahanamoku and Johnny Weissmuller of the United States, but swimming glory was also claimed by athletes from Australia, France, Great Britain, and other countries. Women participated in Olympic swimming beginning in 1912 in Stockholm, Sweden, and soon such female swimmers as Dawn Fraser of Australia and Krisztina Egerszegi of Hungary were inscribing their names in the sport's record books. With each Olympiad, swimming technique, training, and technology have improved, and the world's greatest swimmers have cut through Olympic waters with ever greater speed. As times have been lowered, excitement has been raised, making the pool one of the most thrilling venues for Olympic competition.

ATHENS, GREECE	PARIS, FRANCE	ST. LOUIS, MISSOURI	LONDON, ENGLAND	STOCKHOLM, SWEDEN	ANTWERP, BELGIUM	PARIS, FRANCE	AMSTERDAM, NETHERLANDS	LOS ANGELES, CALIFORNIA	BERLIN, GERMANY	LONDON, ENGLAND	HELSINKI, FINLAND	MELBOURNE, AUSTRALIA	ROME, ITALY	TOKYO, JAPAN	MEXICO CITY, MEXICO	MUNICH, WEST GERMANY	MONTREAL, QUEBEC	MOSCOW, SOVIET UNION	LOS ANGELES, CALIFORNIA	SEOUL, SOUTH KOREA	BARCELONA, SPAIN	ATLANTA, GEORGIA	SYDNEY, AUSTRALIA	ATHENS, GREECE	BEIJING, CHINA	LONDON, ENGLAND
1896	1900	1904	1908	1912	1920	1924	1928	1932	1936	1948	1952	1956	1960	1964	1968	1972	1976	1980	1984	1988	1992	1996	2000	2004	2008	2012

SWIMMING IN THE SEINE

1900 PARIS, FRANCE

The second modern Olympiad was a wild and loosely planned affair. Held over a five-month period that was scheduled to coincide with Paris's World's Fair, the Olympic Games were so under-promoted by organizers that many athletes were uncertain whether they were participating in official Olympic competitions. In the century since, sports historians have been left scratching their heads

Indoor pools were not widespread at the start of the 20th century, leaving early competitions out-of-doors

in attempts to sort out the various sports' results and status. Live pigeon shooting, tug of war, croquet, cricket, and a 200-meter swimming obstacle course *were* official. Ballooning, angling, longue paume (hand tennis), cannon shooting, kite flying, fire fighting, and life saving *were not*.

Conditions for many events were **haphazard**. The track and field competitions were held in a park named Bois de Boulogne on a grassy knoll full of trees. The marathon was so poorly marked and officiated that the fifth-place finisher, American Arthur Newton, claimed he hadn't been passed and that the top two finishers—both Frenchmen whose uniforms were curiously free of mud—had obviously short-cut the course. The swimming competitions were held in the Seine River, a swift-flowing, muddy waterway that cut through the heart of Paris.

The 1900 program for Olympic swimming included a total of 7 events featuring competitors from 12 nations—Australia, Austria, Belgium, Denmark, France, Germany, Great Britain, Hungary, Italy, the Netherlands, Sweden, and the U.S. Of the 76 total competitors, 47 of them were French, though the only gold medalist among them was Charles de Venville, who won the first and only Olympic Underwater Swim contest—an event in which swimmers were given 1 point for each second they remained underwater and 2 points for each meter traveled without stroking. In all, de Venville traveled 60 meters (largely thanks to the current) and remained submerged for 68.4 seconds.

John Arthur Jarvis of Britain took first-place honors in the 1,000-meter and 4,000-meter **freestyle** events. The 4,000-meter race, which Jarvis finished in some 58 minutes—more than 10 minutes ahead of second-place finisher Zoltan Halmay of Hungary—was the longest swimming race in Olympic history for more

Early Olympic medalist John Arthur Jarvis dubbed himself the "amateur swimming champion of the world"

than a century until a 10,000-meter race was introduced in 2008 in Beijing, China. German swimmer Ernst Hoppenberg won the 200-meter **backstroke** and also combined with his countrymen to take top honors in the 4x200-meter freestyle relay.

Fred Lane of Australia, meanwhile, won the individual 200-meter freestyle race as well as perhaps the most interesting swimming event, the 200-meter obstacle swim. In this now defunct race, he bested 9 other swimmers by going over the first 2 obstacles (poles and a row of boats) and under the last (a row of boats) in 2 minutes and 38.4 seconds, edging out silver medalist Otto Wahle of Austria.

Although Pierre de Coubertin—founder of the International Olympic Committee (IOC)—remarked of the Paris Olympics, "It's a miracle the Olympic movement survived these Games," the 1900 Olympiad certainly provided some unique athletic moments that will never again be replicated.

In 1910, a decade after serving as a swimming waterway, a flooded Seine River would devastate Paris

ATHENS, GREECE	PARIS, FRANCE	ST. LOUIS, MISSOURI	LONDON, ENGLAND	**STOCKHOLM, SWEDEN**	**ANTWERP, BELGIUM**	**PARIS, FRANCE**	AMSTERDAM, NETHERLANDS	LOS ANGELES, CALIFORNIA	**BERLIN, GERMANY**	LONDON, ENGLAND	HELSINKI, FINLAND	MELBOURNE, AUSTRALIA	ROME, ITALY	TOKYO, JAPAN	MEXICO CITY, MEXICO	MUNICH, WEST GERMANY	MONTREAL, QUEBEC	MOSCOW, SOVIET UNION	LOS ANGELES, CALIFORNIA	SEOUL, SOUTH KOREA	BARCELONA, SPAIN	ATLANTA, GEORGIA	SYDNEY, AUSTRALIA	ATHENS, GREECE	BEIJING, CHINA	LONDON, ENGLAND
1896	1900	1904	1908	1912	1920	1924	1928	1932	1936	1948	1952	1956	1960	1964	1968	1972	1976	1980	1984	1988	1992	1996	2000	2004	2008	2012

THE GRAND DUKE

DUKE KAHANAMOKU U.S. EVENTS: 100-METER FREESTYLE, 4X200-METER FREESTYLE RELAY

OLYMPIC COMPETITIONS: 1912, 1920, 1924

At a 1911 **amateur** swim meet in Honolulu Harbor, 21-year-old Duke Kahanamoku of Hawaii set what appeared to be world records in the 50-yard and 100-yard races. The records were disallowed by the **Amateur Athletic Union (AAU),** which attributed the fast times to the tide's aiding swimmers and to poor timing methods. But Kahanamoku removed any doubt that he was a world-class swimmer at the 1912 Olympic Games in Stockholm, Sweden. There, he won the 100-meter freestyle gold medal for the U.S. in world-record time and took silver as a part of the 4x200-meter relay team.

In the years that followed—including 1916, when the Olympics slated to be held in Berlin, Germany, were canceled due to war—"The Duke" found great celebrity by giving many exhibitions in

Hawaiian Duke Kahanamoku loved warm waters, once saying, "I do not know what winter means"

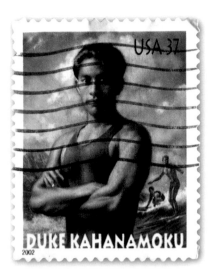

swimming as well as in another of his passions: surfing. In fact, thanks to Kahanamoku's performance at a 1915 surfing exhibition in Australia, the sport of surfing's popularity grew to unforeseen levels, and Australians dubbed Kahanamoku "The Father of Modern Surfing."

When the Olympics resumed in Antwerp, Belgium, in 1920, Kahanamoku was there and in rare form despite dreary, cold weather and a subpar swimming facility. "The swimming and diving were held in part of an old moat," recalled Alice Landon, a member of the U.S. women's diving team. "It was the clammiest, darkest place, and the water was frigid. It looked bottomless and black." Kahanamoku's main competitor in Antwerp's cold, dark waters was fellow American Norman Ross, but the Hawaiian—swimming the 100-meter freestyle finals on August 24, 1920, his 30th birthday—set the world record with a time of 60.4 seconds to easily win gold. Kahanamoku also teamed up with Ross, Perry McGillivray, and Pua Kealoha to win the 4x200-meter relay gold medal in a world-record time of 10:04.

But Kahanamoku's Olympic career was not yet finished. In 1924, he made the U.S. swim team as a gold-medal threat in the 100-meter freestyle. In the finals, Kahanamoku swam a thrilling race against his 21-year-old brother Sam and new American swimming sensation Johnny Weissmuller (who later would gain fame by portraying Tarzan in a series of Hollywood films). Although the Kahanamoku brothers gave him a run, Weissmuller pulled away and won the race in an Olympic-record 59 seconds flat.

Although Kahanamoku's Olympic career had ended, his accomplishments in the water had not. On June 14, 1925, Kahanamoku helped save eight drowning sailors from a sinking ship off the coast of Newport Beach, California, by ferrying them one at a time to dry land on his surfboard. He went on to appear in a number of Hollywood movies himself and is today memorialized with a statue on Waikiki Beach near Honolulu.

In a fitting sendoff, Kahanamoku's ashes were scattered in the Pacific Ocean after his death in 1968

ATHENS, GREECE — 1896
PARIS, FRANCE — 1900
ST. LOUIS, MISSOURI — 1904
LONDON, ENGLAND — 1908
STOCKHOLM, SWEDEN — 1912
ANTWERP, BELGIUM — 1920
PARIS, FRANCE — 1924
AMSTERDAM, NETHERLANDS — 1928
LOS ANGELES, CALIFORNIA — 1932
BERLIN, GERMANY — 1936
LONDON, ENGLAND — 1948
HELSINKI, FINLAND — 1952
MELBOURNE, AUSTRALIA — 1956
ROME, ITALY — 1960
TOKYO, JAPAN — 1964
MEXICO CITY, MEXICO — 1968
MUNICH, WEST GERMANY — 1972
MONTREAL, QUEBEC — 1976
MOSCOW, SOVIET UNION — 1980
LOS ANGELES, CALIFORNIA — 1984
SEOUL, SOUTH KOREA — 1988
BARCELONA, SPAIN — 1992
ATLANTA, GEORGIA — 1996
SYDNEY, AUSTRALIA — 2000
ATHENS, GREECE — 2004
BEIJING, CHINA — 2008
LONDON, ENGLAND — 2012

THE DAWN OF AUSTRALIAN SWIMMING

DAWN FRASER   AUSTRALIA   EVENTS: 100-METER FREESTYLE, 400-METER FREESTYLE, 4X100-METER

FREESTYLE RELAY, 4X100-METER MEDLEY RELAY   OLYMPIC COMPETITIONS: 1956, 1960, 1964

Raised as the youngest of eight children in the Sydney suburb of Balmain, Dawn Fraser took up swimming because it was inexpensive, pools and water were plentiful in the swimming-mad

In 1998, long after her retirement, Dawn Fraser was voted the greatest female athlete in Australia's history

Australia of her youth, and the exercise helped remedy her **asthma**. Soon she was discovered by swimming coach Harry Gallagher. "She had wild aggression," said Gallagher. "She reminded me of a wild mare in the hills that you had to put the lightest lead on to keep her under control. She wanted to do her own thing. If you had to guide her, it had to be very subtly, so she didn't understand that she was being manipulated."

Gallagher's training methods—which included racing Fraser against top male swimmers—worked well, and by February 1956, Fraser had set a world record in the 100-meter freestyle. At the 1956 Olympics, Fraser reset the world record in that event to win gold. In 1960, the Australian sensation repeated as champion in the 100-meter freestyle in world-record–breaking time but angered her teammates by refusing to swim in a qualifying **heat** of the 4x100-meter **medley** relay because she had just finished lunch. She did swim in the finals of the medley relay and helped her team capture silver, but her behavior had hurt her standing with the Australian Swimming Union (ASU).

In February 1964, Fraser broke the 100-meter freestyle world record for the 11th and final time. Eight days later, her world was shattered when she was the driver in an automobile accident that killed her mother and left her in a steel back brace with chipped vertebrae in her neck. Amazingly, Fraser put herself back together mentally and physically in time to again win gold in the 100-meter freestyle in the 1964 Tokyo Olympics. But a bizarre occurrence there effectively ended Fraser's swimming career while contributing to her reputation as a "larrikin"—an Australian term for a rowdy or mischievous person.

According to police reports, Fraser had swum the moat surrounding Japanese emperor Hirohito's palace in order to steal the Japanese flag and fly an Olympic flag in its place. Fraser was arrested but released without

charge, and the emperor even gave Fraser the flag she sought as a gift. But the ASU banned her from further competition following the Olympics. Fraser maintained that she was innocent of the allegations, saying, "There's no way I would have swum in that moat. I was terrified of dirty water, and that moat was filthy. There's no way I'd have dipped my toe in it."

Although the ASU lifted her ban just prior to the 1968 Games, Fraser had not trained and so did not compete. She did, however, go on to serve in Australian parliament for a short while and was selected as a torch bearer at the opening ceremonies of the 2000 Olympic Games, hosted by Sydney.

In 1963, Fraser (pictured, without cap) became the first woman to swim 100 meters in less than a minute

ATHENS, GREECE	PARIS, FRANCE	ST. LOUIS, MISSOURI	LONDON, ENGLAND	STOCKHOLM, SWEDEN	ANTWERP, BELGIUM	PARIS, FRANCE	AMSTERDAM, NETHERLANDS	LOS ANGELES, CALIFORNIA	BERLIN, GERMANY	LONDON, ENGLAND	HELSINKI, FINLAND	MELBOURNE, AUSTRALIA	ROME, ITALY	TOKYO, JAPAN	**MEXICO CITY, MEXICO**	**MUNICH, WEST GERMANY**	MONTREAL, QUEBEC	MOSCOW, SOVIET UNION	LOS ANGELES, CALIFORNIA	SEOUL, SOUTH KOREA	BARCELONA, SPAIN	ATLANTA, GEORGIA	SYDNEY, AUSTRALIA	ATHENS, GREECE	BEIJING, CHINA	LONDON, ENGLAND
1896	1900	1904	1908	1912	1920	1924	1928	1932	1936	1948	1952	1956	1960	1964	**1968**	**1972**	1976	1980	1984	1988	1992	1996	2000	2004	2008	2012

MARK THE SHARK

MARK SPITZ U.S. EVENTS: 100-METER BUTTERFLY, 100-METER FREESTYLE, 200-METER BUTTERFLY, 200-METER FREESTYLE, 4X100-METER FREESTYLE RELAY, 4X100-METER MEDLEY RELAY, 4X200-METER FREESTYLE RELAY OLYMPIC COMPETITIONS: 1968, 1972

In Mexico City in 1968, 18-year-old American Mark Spitz was expected to make his mark in the Olympic swimming history books by winning six gold medals. It was a tall order, but the confident youngster had brought the pressure upon himself by publicly predicting the feat. Although he won

Although most swimmers shave all body hair, Mark Spitz kept his mustache as a gesture of rebellion

two gold medals as a part of both the 4x100-meter and 4x200-meter freestyle relay teams, Spitz failed to win any of the individual events, finishing second in the 100-meter **butterfly**, third in the 100-meter freestyle, and eighth in the 200-meter butterfly. Because Spitz finished second to fellow American Doug Russell in the 100-meter butterfly, he lost the opportunity to compete on the 4x100-meter medley relay team, which captured gold.

Although many athletes wouldn't consider two golds, a silver, and a bronze a disappointing medal haul from one Olympiad, Spitz did. After all, he was the world-record holder in the 100- and 200-meter butterfly yet didn't win those races in Mexico City. The disappointment lit a fire in Spitz, prompting him to work even harder, and he went into intense training under the tutelage of American Olympic swim coach Doc Counsilman while attending Indiana University.

By the time 1972 rolled around, Spitz was a swimming machine. Nicknamed "Mark the Shark," he tore through the water in competitions leading up to the Olympic Games, setting world records in each of the seven events he was entered to swim in Munich, West Germany.

Once at the Munich Games, Spitz again attacked the world record books, writing his name in bold strokes. When all was said and done, Spitz—sporting a trademark mustache that helped turn him into something of a heartthrob among female fans in the U.S.—had won seven gold medals, each in world-record time. Four of Spitz's golds came in individual competition (the 100- and 200-meter freestyle and 100- and 200-meter butterfly), while the others came as part of relay teams (the 4x100- and 4x200-meter freestyle relays and 4x100-meter medley relay). Spitz retired from swimming after the 1972 Games and later worked as a TV announcer before settling down to raise a family.

No swimmer approached Spitz's standard of Olympic excellence until American phenom Michael Phelps showed up in 2008 at the Olympic pool in Beijing, China, and won eight golds in eight

Before shooting to stardom as a swimmer, Mark Spitz hoped to become a dentist. After ending his athletic career, he got into television acting and sports broadcasting.

Spitz was honored with the title "World Swimmer of the Year" three times—in 1969, 1971, and 1972

Sports Illustrated

SEPTEMBER 4, 1972   60 CENTS

OLYMPIAN MARK SPITZ

events—all but one in world-record time. Many wondered what Spitz's reaction would be to Phelps's performance, and although Spitz initially felt slighted that he had not been invited by the U.S. Olympic Committee to watch the 2008 Olympics in person, he was gracious toward Phelps. "I feel a tremendous load off my back," he said. "Somebody told me years ago you judge one's character by the company you keep, and I'm just happy to be in the company of Michael Phelps. I'm so proud of what he's been able to do. I did what I did, and it was in my day in those set of circumstances. For 36 years, it stood as a benchmark."

Spitz and two of his teammates celebrate in 1972 after claiming gold in the 4x100-meter medley relay

ATHENS, GREECE	PARIS, FRANCE	ST. LOUIS, MISSOURI	LONDON, ENGLAND	STOCKHOLM, SWEDEN	ANTWERP, BELGIUM	PARIS, FRANCE	AMSTERDAM, NETHERLANDS	LOS ANGELES, CALIFORNIA	BERLIN, GERMANY	LONDON, ENGLAND	HELSINKI, FINLAND	MELBOURNE, AUSTRALIA	ROME, ITALY	TOKYO, JAPAN	MEXICO CITY, MEXICO	MUNICH, WEST GERMANY	MONTREAL, QUEBEC	MOSCOW, SOVIET UNION	LOS ANGELES, CALIFORNIA	SEOUL, SOUTH KOREA	BARCELONA, SPAIN	ATLANTA, GEORGIA	SYDNEY, AUSTRALIA	ATHENS, GREECE	BEIJING, CHINA	LONDON, ENGLAND
1896	1900	1904	1908	1912	1920	1924	1928	1932	1936	1948	1952	1956	1960	1964	1968	1972	1976	1980	1984	1988	1992	1996	2000	2004	2008	2012

COUNTERFEIT DEUTSCHE MARKS

EAST GERMAN WOMEN'S SWIMMING 1976, 1980, 1984, 1988

Seventeen-year-old Kornelia Ender of East Germany broke onto the Olympic swimming scene in 1976 in Montreal, Quebec, winning four gold medals in world-record time. Ender had swum at the 1972 Olympics in Munich, winning 3 silver medals as a 13-year-old, and had trained hard for 1976. But the 18 pounds of muscle she gained in the months prior to the Montreal Games surprised her even more than the 4 gold medals she won there—or the 11 total gold medals that East Germany won in women's swimming events. "They were very strong women," said Wendy Boglioli, captain of the 1976 U.S. women's Olympic swim team. "They were very fast. We thought they were machines."

In 1980, in Moscow, Soviet Union, Rica Reinisch became the next East German female swimmer to win Olympic gold—setting multiple world records. Reinisch was just 15 at the time, and her rise to Olympic glory was remarkably quick and intense. How did she get so good so fast? And how, moreover, did the East German women as a whole start dominating world swimming? In addition to a nationalistic craze for sports training, the East Germans

Rica Reinisch found fame in 1980 but later felt betrayed by her country

were taking supplements. "We usually got the tablets after very hard water training sessions," said Reinisch. "Vitamin C, vitamin B, potassium, calcium, magnesium, all kinds of pills. It was a real cupful."

Unbeknownst to at least some of the swimmers themselves, part of this "vitamin" dosage was actually Oral Turinabol, a **steroid** commonly called "OT." OT contains testosterone, which occurs naturally in the male body and increases muscle mass and shortens recovery time while also causing voice deepening and hair growth. Following the Moscow Olympics, Reinisch saw a doctor who told her and her parents that her ovaries—the reproductive organs responsible for producing eggs—showed signs of damage. Reinisch's mother withdrew her daughter from the East German swimming program. In the years that followed, Reinisch developed heart trouble and had two miscarriages before finally giving birth to two healthy children.

East Germany's final *wundermädchen* (German for "wondergirl") was Kristin Otto, who won six gold medals in 1988, the highest total ever achieved at one Olympiad by a woman. But when the Berlin Wall came tumbling down in 1989, setting into motion events that soon

united Germany under one democratic republic and made obsolete the **communism** of East Germany, records of East German doping were uncovered, mostly due to the extensive record-keeping of the Stasi, the state's security service. "Doping in the GDR [East Germany] was different than the doping in the rest of the world, but it was also different than the doping in the other parts of the East," said Werner Franke, a German doctor. "It was German. It was orderly. It was **bureaucratic**. It was written up."

Despite these findings, not all East German Olympic athletes admitted to cheating, and it was left unclear which athletes knew of the systematic doping and which did not. "I won't allege that anyone took anything," said Petra Thümer, who won two swimming gold medals in the 1976 Games, 30 years later. "I won't let anyone take this success away from me, this hard-won success. I spent many years in performance sports. I loved swimming and to work hard for it."

> **"They were very fast. We thought they were machines."** – *Wendy Boglioli*

East German swimmer Kristin Otto's six gold medals in the 1988 Games stunned the sports world

ATHENS, GREECE — 1896
PARIS, FRANCE — 1900
ST. LOUIS, MISSOURI — 1904
LONDON, ENGLAND — 1908
STOCKHOLM, SWEDEN — 1912
ANTWERP, BELGIUM — 1920
PARIS, FRANCE — 1924
AMSTERDAM, NETHERLANDS — 1928
LOS ANGELES, CALIFORNIA — 1932
BERLIN, GERMANY — 1936
LONDON, ENGLAND — 1948
HELSINKI, FINLAND — 1952
MELBOURNE, AUSTRALIA — 1956
ROME, ITALY — 1960
TOKYO, JAPAN — 1964
MEXICO CITY, MEXICO — 1968
MUNICH, WEST GERMANY — 1972
MONTREAL, QUEBEC — 1976
MOSCOW, SOVIET UNION — 1980
LOS ANGELES, CALIFORNIA — 1984
SEOUL, SOUTH KOREA — 1988
BARCELONA, SPAIN — 1992
ATLANTA, GEORGIA — 1996
SYDNEY, AUSTRALIA — 2000
ATHENS, GREECE — 2004
BEIJING, CHINA — 2008
LONDON, ENGLAND — 2012

SWIMMING LIKE THE DOLPHINS

1988 SEOUL, SOUTH KOREA

One of the fastest swimmers in the ocean is the dolphin. It is of little surprise, then, that world-class swimmers, in their ceaseless attempts to lower their racing times, would look to these speedy sea creatures for new innovations in human swimming techniques.

Swimmers have long studied dolphins for their swimming movements and means of propulsion

By 1988, American backstroker David Berkoff had made the **undulating** kick of the dolphin an integral part of his own swimming repertoire. By starting the first 25 meters of a race underwater and kicking like a dolphin, Berkoff would pop to the surface in the lead and then hold on for victory. Berkoff's method became so successful that it was nicknamed the "Berkoff Blastoff" and enabled him to set the world record in the 100-meter backstroke in the U.S. Olympic Trials in early 1988. "It seemed pretty obvious to me that kicking underwater seemed to be a lot faster than swimming on the surface," said Berkoff, who later admitted that without the dolphin kick he "probably wouldn't have made the Olympic team. I probably would have been a good backstroker but not a great one. [The dolphin kick] was something that really kind of changed the way the backstroke was swum."

Going into the 1988 Olympics in Seoul, South Korea, Berkoff was considered the heavy favorite to take gold in the 100-meter backstroke. But lying in wait was Japanese swimmer Daichi Suzuki, who had been experimenting with the dolphin kick himself—with less success than Berkoff—for nearly a decade. Suzuki had taken notes from Puerto Rican swimmer Jesse Vassallo—another early innovator of the dolphin kick—and though he trained in relative obscurity, by the start of the 1988 Games, he was ready to shock the swimming world.

On the morning of September 24, 1988, Berkoff was at his best in the **prelims** of the 100-meter backstroke, breaking his old world record of 54.91 seconds with a time of 54.51. Suzuki came in a distant third at 55.90. But the finals, held later that night, were a different story. Suzuki bettered Berkoff's Blastoff with an amazing start that kept him underwater and dolphin-kicking for a full 35 meters and 15 seconds, longer than he ever had, and put him just ahead of Berkoff. The prevailing opinion was that it was folly for a swimmer to hold his

breath for such a long period while physically exerting himself. Suzuki and Berkoff defied this logic. After such explosive starts, only 15 meters, a **flip turn** at the wall, and 50 meters of homestretch remained, which Suzuki attacked like he never had before, winning gold with a time of 55.05, just ahead of Berkoff's second-place 55.18. One week after the 1988 Games, IOC officials instituted a new rule that forced backstrokers to surface within the first 15 meters of the starting wall.

Daichi Suzuki won gold with a combination of strong lungs and extensive swimming experimentation

	1896	1900	1904	1908	1912	1920	1924	1928	1932	1936	1948	1952	1956	1960	1964	1968	1972	1976	1980	**1984**	**1988**	**1992**	1996	2000	2004	2008	2012
	ATHENS, GREECE	PARIS, FRANCE	ST. LOUIS, MISSOURI	LONDON, ENGLAND	STOCKHOLM, SWEDEN	ANTWERP, BELGIUM	PARIS, FRANCE	AMSTERDAM, NETHERLANDS	LOS ANGELES, CALIFORNIA	BERLIN, GERMANY	LONDON, ENGLAND	HELSINKI, FINLAND	MELBOURNE, AUSTRALIA	ROME, ITALY	TOKYO, JAPAN	MEXICO CITY, MEXICO	MUNICH, WEST GERMANY	MONTREAL, QUEBEC	MOSCOW, SOVIET UNION	**LOS ANGELES, CALIFORNIA**	**SEOUL, SOUTH KOREA**	**BARCELONA, SPAIN**	ATLANTA, GEORGIA	SYDNEY, AUSTRALIA	ATHENS, GREECE	BEIJING, CHINA	LONDON, ENGLAND

FLAWLESS

MATT BIONDI U.S. EVENTS: 50-METER FREESTYLE, 100-METER FREESTYLE, 200-METER FREESTYLE, 100-METER BUTTERFLY, 200-METER BUTTERFLY, 4X100-METER FREESTYLE RELAY, 4X100-METER MEDLEY RELAY, 4X200-METER FREESTYLE RELAY

OLYMPIC COMPETITIONS: 1984, 1988, 1992

In 1988, American swimmer Matt Biondi became only the second man in Olympic history to nab seven medals in one Olympics, winning five golds, a silver, and a bronze. But for Biondi, a 6–foot–6

Matt Biondi helped develop his explosive speed by playing water polo in his teenage and college years

swimming specimen renowned for his flawless stroke, Olympic competition—
and swimming in general—was more about the experience than the medals.

In 1984, at the age of 18, Biondi had won Olympic gold in world-record
time as part of the 4x100-meter freestyle relay team at the Los Angeles
Games. By 1988, Biondi was being heralded by the American press as the next
Mark Spitz and was expected to equal or surpass Spitz's legendary medal haul.

Biondi was never comfortable with the public projections, and he
kept a journal for *Sports Illustrated* during the 1988 Games that showed his
displeasure with what he deemed negative and unfair expectations from the
media. In it, he wrote: "I'm doing this diary because I want to voice the other
side of the Olympics. Everyone will be counting the medals and the times
and the world records, and making this big judgment: Is Matt a success or a
failure? It seems there's so much emphasis put on that stuff and so little on
how a person grows as he works his way toward the Olympics. To me, it's the
path getting there that counts, not the cheese at the end of the maze."

The pressure was heightened after Biondi's opening event in Seoul,
in which any hopes of winning seven gold medals were dashed when he
swam what he felt was a satisfying race but took bronze in the 200-meter
freestyle. The scrutiny increased when he was nipped at the finish in the
100-meter butterfly by Anthony Nesty of Suriname; the American fell a
hundredth of a second short because he had miscalculated the final wall and
glided—rather than stroked—to the finish. Biondi was aggravated by the loss
but said, through his journal, "After all, what's a one-hundredth of a second?
Could I have won with longer fingernails? A slightly quicker start? Looking
at the tape of the race just makes me sick to my stomach. But at least I've
improved from bronze to silver."

Biondi's fortunes, and swimming, then improved. He won his first gold of the 1988 Games as part of the 4x200-meter freestyle relay team. Then the gold medals began to come to Biondi as effortlessly as his flawless strokes. The 100-meter freestyle, 4x100-meter freestyle relay, 50-meter freestyle, and 4x100-meter medley relay all ended in gold for Biondi. Although he vowed to retire following the 1988 Games, Biondi was lured back to the Olympic pool for the 1992 Games in Barcelona, where he picked up three more medals and enjoyed a final taste of the Olympic experience.

After medaling in three Olympics, Biondi earned an education degree and became a math teacher

ATHENS, GREECE	PARIS, FRANCE	ST. LOUIS, MISSOURI	LONDON, ENGLAND	STOCKHOLM, SWEDEN	ANTWERP, BELGIUM	PARIS, FRANCE	AMSTERDAM, NETHERLANDS	LOS ANGELES, CALIFORNIA	BERLIN, GERMANY	LONDON, ENGLAND	HELSINKI, FINLAND	MELBOURNE, AUSTRALIA	ROME, ITALY	TOKYO, JAPAN	MEXICO CITY, MEXICO	MUNICH, WEST GERMANY	MONTREAL, QUEBEC	MOSCOW, SOVIET UNION	LOS ANGELES, CALIFORNIA	SEOUL, SOUTH KOREA	BARCELONA, SPAIN	ATLANTA, GEORGIA	SYDNEY, AUSTRALIA	ATHENS, GREECE	BEIJING, CHINA	LONDON, ENGLAND
1896	1900	1904	1908	1912	1920	1924	1928	1932	1936	1948	1952	1956	1960	1964	1968	1972	1976	1980	1984	1988	1992	1996	2000	2004	2008	2012

THORPEDO ROCKS THE POOL

IAN THORPE AUSTRALIA EVENTS: 100-METER FREESTYLE, 200-METER FREESTYLE,
400-METER FREESTYLE, 4X100-METER FREESTYLE RELAY, 4X100-METER MEDLEY RELAY
4X200-METER FREESTYLE RELAY OLYMPIC COMPETITIONS: 2000, 2004

He had feet like flippers and hands like oars. He had the propulsion of a dolphin and the instinct of a killer whale. He was only 17 years old but already had the nickname—"The Thorpedo"—of a

Ian Thorpe's ascent to stardom was perfectly timed, coinciding with his country's second hosted Olympiad

superhero. He had the popularity of a rock star in a country that was cuckoo for its swimmers, and he was competing in the world's preeminent, once-every-four-years sporting gala. His name was Ian Thorpe. The gala was the Sydney Olympic Games.

Thorpe was the son of accomplished athletes—his mother and father were skilled **netball** and **cricket** players respectively. Young Ian, though, showed a natural talent for swimming and made a splash in world-class competition as a 16-year-old, setting world records in the 200- and 400-meter freestyle races. The Australian public, which was already high on sports with its preparations as an Olympic host in 2000, went wild with anticipation. In May 2000 at the Australian Olympic qualifying meet, Thorpe set new world records in both the 200- and 400-meter freestyle races.

Thorpe's pool performance in the 2000 Olympics netted him five medals, including three golds. But no medal—or experience, for that matter—was more valuable to Thorpe than the gold he and countrymen Michael Klim, Chris Fydler, and Ashley Callus won on the first day of competition in the 4x100-meter freestyle relay. Before 2000, the U.S. men's team had never lost the 4x100-meter freestyle relay in Olympic competition, and its **anchor** swimmer in 2000, Gary Hall Jr., publicly proclaimed that that would not change in Sydney, despite Australia's talented collection of swimmers. "My biased opinion says that we will smash [the Australians] like guitars," Hall said. "Historically, the U.S. has always risen to the occasion."

The race went down as one of the most thrilling in the annals of Olympic swimming. The Americans and Australians traded the lead through the first three **legs**, and Thorpe hit the pool slightly ahead of Hall. Thorpe lost the lead in the first 50 meters as Hall went all-out early. After the race's

last flip turn, the rivals stroked down the final 50-meter stretch nearly even. But with about 15 meters to go, the Thorpedo surged ahead as if he were riding a wave and hit the wall first. The Aussies' time was 3:13.67, nineteen-one-hundredths of a second faster than the Americans', and a new world record by nearly a second and a half.

The Australian victory sent the fans into a frenzy, and all four Australian swimmers were soon on the **deck**, acknowledging the crowd and even playing air guitar in mockery of Hall's "guitar smashing" statement. "This was the best day of my life," Thorpe said. "This was the best hour of my life. These were the best minutes of my life. I'm pleased I'm one of the few athletes who have performed at their best in an Olympics. I've researched that. The statistics are slim, the number of athletes who have performed at their best in the Olympics."

The men's 4x100-meter freestyle relay may have been Australia's proudest moment of the Sydney Games

ATHENS, GREECE 1896
PARIS, FRANCE 1900
ST. LOUIS, MISSOURI 1904
LONDON, ENGLAND 1908
STOCKHOLM, SWEDEN 1912
ANTWERP, BELGIUM 1920
PARIS, FRANCE 1924
AMSTERDAM, NETHERLANDS 1928
LOS ANGELES, CALIFORNIA 1932
BERLIN, GERMANY 1936
LONDON, ENGLAND 1948
HELSINKI, FINLAND 1952
MELBOURNE, AUSTRALIA 1956
ROME, ITALY 1960
TOKYO, JAPAN 1964
MEXICO CITY, MEXICO 1968
MUNICH, WEST GERMANY 1972
MONTREAL, QUEBEC 1976
MOSCOW, SOVIET UNION 1980
LOS ANGELES, CALIFORNIA 1984
SEOUL, SOUTH KOREA 1988
BARCELONA, SPAIN 1992
ATLANTA, GEORGIA 1996
SYDNEY, AUSTRALIA 2000
ATHENS, GREECE 2004
BEIJING, CHINA 2008
LONDON, ENGLAND 2012

ERIC THE EEL

2000 SYDNEY, AUSTRALIA

On September 19 at the 2000 Olympics in Sydney, Pieter van den Hoogenband of the Netherlands set a new world record of 47.84 seconds in a preliminary heat of the 100-meter freestyle race, beating such elite swimmers as American speedster Gary Hall Jr. But in that day's first 100-meter freestyle heat, one swimmer created his own unforgettable moment and drew even

Eric Moussambani's swim in the 2000 Games turned out to be a lonely but unforgettable experience

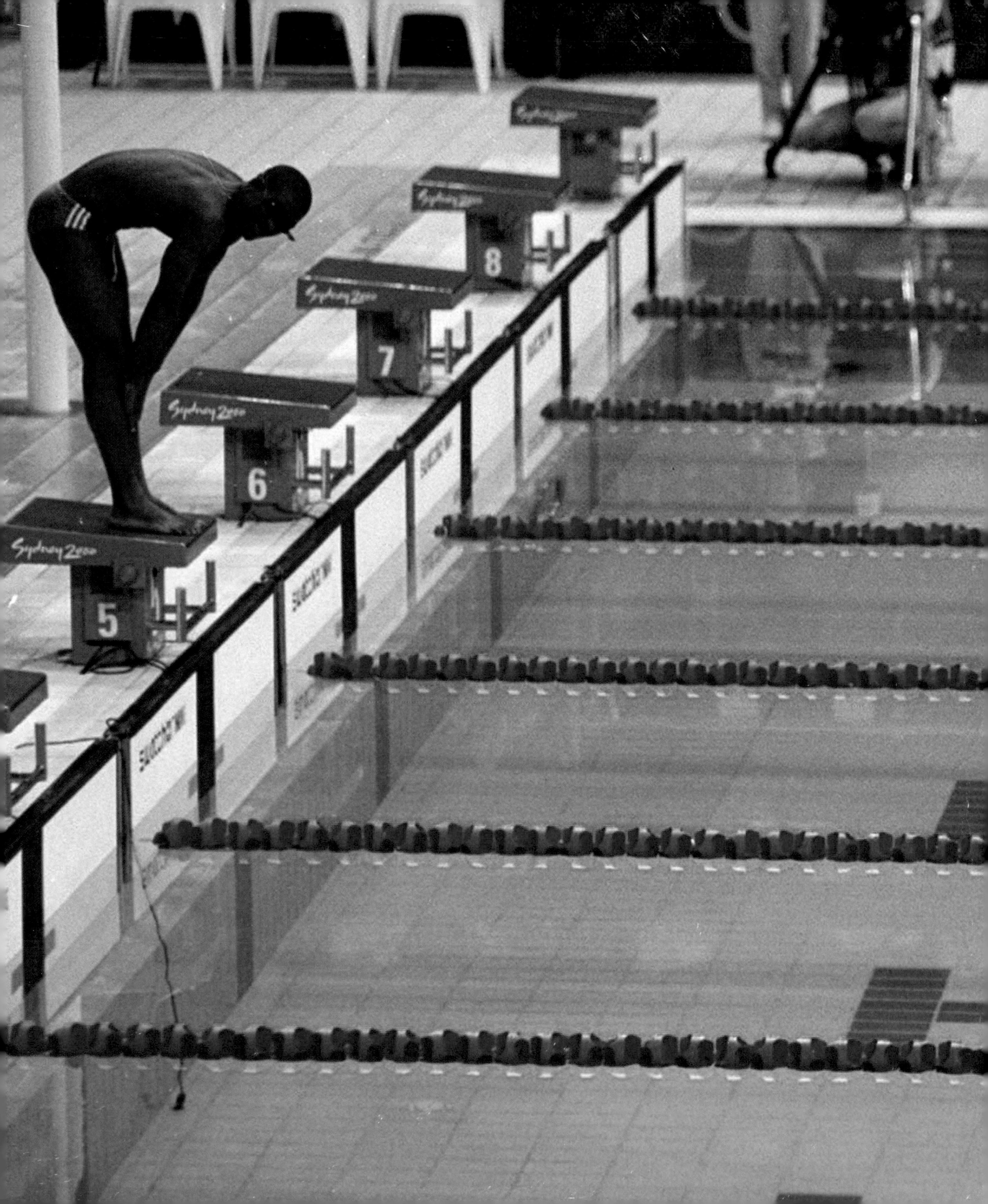
Sydney 2000
8
7
6
5

more heartfelt cheers than the new world-record holder.

In the opening heat of the 100-meter freestyle, Eric Moussambani of Equatorial Guinea took to the starting blocks, lined up next to Karim Bare of Nigeria and Farkhod Oripov of Tajikistan. These three swimmers gained entrance to the Games not by way of their qualifying times but by invitation from IOC president Juan Antonio Samaranch, who chose a handful of athletes from some of the world's **developing nations** in the interest of promoting the value of sport. As the three swimmers readied for the start, Bare and Oripov teetered on the blocks and fell into the pool before the **starter's mark**, leaving them both disqualified for false starts. Although the fans booed, rules were rules, and now only Moussambani remained.

Again taking the blocks—the drawstring dangling untied on the outside of his simple, royal blue swim trunks—the rigidly muscular, 5-foot-7 Moussambani recrouched. At the starter's mark, he dove into the water cleanly, even executing a few underwater dolphin kicks. Moussambani then began furiously paddling for the opposite wall with wild strokes that looked more like aquatic boxing than the **crawl stroke**.

Unfortunately, "Eric the Eel," as he was later dubbed, had obviously spent himself in the first 50 meters, and, after an awkward flip turn at the wall, his strokes became more labored. The final 25 meters were an all-out struggle for the exhausted swimmer, but the volume of the crowd swelled, urging Moussambani onward down the final portion of the homestretch. Although Moussambani's stroke was now virtually all arms—his nearly lifeless legs having sunk beneath him—he windmilled a couple more strokes to reach the wall for a time of 1:52.72.

Moussambani's time was a full minute slower than what the medalists' marks would be later in the competition, but he was happy with his effort and touched by the reception from the fans in attendance. "I want to send hugs and kisses to the crowd," he said. "It was their cheering that kept me going. I'm really pleased with what happened. Gold medals are not everything at the Olympic Games.

> **"Gold medals are not everything at the Olympic Games. What happened to me was worth more than gold."**
> – Eric Moussambani

What happened to me was worth more than gold. I want to train now and come back in Athens in 2004."

Unfortunately for Moussambani, the Equatorial Guinea Olympic Committee failed to properly register him for the 2004 Olympics, claiming that it could not find his passport photo. It was a great disappointment to Moussambani, who spent his time following the Sydney Games touring Europe with the apparel company Speedo to promote swimming. He also continued with his training, reportedly lowering his 100-meter times to less than 57 seconds.

Moussambani won the crowd over with his effort, later admitting, "the last 15 meters were very difficult"

ATHENS, GREECE 1896
PARIS, FRANCE 1900
ST. LOUIS, MISSOURI 1904
LONDON, ENGLAND 1908
STOCKHOLM, SWEDEN 1912
ANTWERP, BELGIUM 1920
PARIS, FRANCE 1924
AMSTERDAM, NETHERLANDS 1928
LOS ANGELES, CALIFORNIA 1932
BERLIN, GERMANY 1936
LONDON, ENGLAND 1948
HELSINKI, FINLAND 1952
MELBOURNE, AUSTRALIA 1956
ROME, ITALY 1960
TOKYO, JAPAN 1964
MEXICO CITY, MEXICO 1968
MUNICH, WEST GERMANY 1972
MONTREAL, QUEBEC 1976
MOSCOW, SOVIET UNION 1980
LOS ANGELES, CALIFORNIA 1984
SEOUL, SOUTH KOREA 1988
BARCELONA, SPAIN 1992
ATLANTA, GEORGIA 1996
SYDNEY, AUSTRALIA 2000
ATHENS, GREECE 2004
BEIJING, CHINA 2008
LONDON, ENGLAND 2012

TOUCH OF GOLD

2008 BEIJING, CHINA

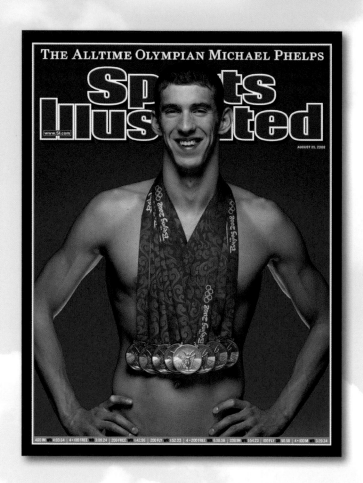

In 2008 in Beijing, American swimmer Michael Phelps enjoyed arguably the greatest Olympics of any athlete in history. By winning eight gold medals while competing in eight events, Phelps surpassed the efforts of U.S. swimmer Mark Spitz, who took seven golds away from the 1972 Olympics in Munich. But Phelps wouldn't have eclipsed Spitz's record without

Thanks to his 2008 medal haul, Michael Phelps was named Sports Illustrated's *"Sportsman of the Year"*

eclipsing Milorad Cavic of Serbia to win the 100-meter butterfly, and he very nearly didn't.

The 100-meter butterfly was Phelps's seventh event of the 2008 Olympics, and in his previous six events, he had won six golds and captured the attention of the entire sports world. Before the race, in a moment of personal preparation, Phelps stood to the side of his starting block in lane five with his right foot resting on the block as he stared straight ahead. Curiously, Cavic decided to mirror Phelps's stance by doing the same thing in lane four, facing Phelps. Was it some sort of mind game or an attempt at intimidation? "I definitely wasn't staring him down," Cavic later said. "I was just trying to control my energy. Both of us have metallic goggles, so I couldn't see his eyes and he couldn't see mine. Maybe he saw his reflection in my goggles and said, 'Hey, I look pretty good.'"

Phelps, however, was not looking good after the first 50 meters of the race. In the 100-meter race, which consisted of one length down and one length back at the Chinese aquatics facility nicknamed "The Water Cube," fans gasped as Phelps flip-turned at the wall in seventh place out of eight competitors. The blazing Cavic hit the halfway mark in first place. Knowledgeable swimming fans, though, knew that Phelps had a reputation for slow starts and strong finishes.

As Phelps began to eat up the distance between himself and the leaders, the crowd in the Water Cube roared. But with just 25 meters left, and then just 10, Cavic still held the lead and looked to be the victor. Phelps then came on furiously, though, and with a final half-stroke out-touched a gliding Cavic at the wall. Whipping off his goggles, Phelps looked at the official scoreboard and saw that he had beaten Cavic by

a scant one-hundredth of a second—50.58 to 50.59. Racing officials then examined video and photographic evidence to be certain that Phelps had won in response to a Serbian inquiry before calling Phelps the official winner. "When I took that last stroke," said Phelps, "I thought I lost the race there, but it turns out that was the difference." Phelps went on to break Spitz's mark of seven golds by winning his eighth in the 4x100-meter medley relay the next day.

Cavic, meanwhile, was honored by a visit with Serbian prime minister Vojislav Kostunica, who praised the swimmer for his strong challenge. "I didn't beat Phelps," said Cavic. "Perhaps I was the only guy at this competition who had a real shot at beating Phelps one-on-one."

Phelps (opposite) reacts after winning the 100-meter butterfly final by the smallest of margins (above)

Phelps had the perfect swimmer's build, with huge hands and feet, long arms, and unusual flexibility

ATHENS, GREECE	PARIS, FRANCE	ST. LOUIS, MISSOURI	LONDON, ENGLAND	STOCKHOLM, SWEDEN	ANTWERP, BELGIUM	PARIS, FRANCE	AMSTERDAM, NETHERLANDS	LOS ANGELES, CALIFORNIA	BERLIN, GERMANY	LONDON, ENGLAND	HELSINKI, FINLAND	MELBOURNE, AUSTRALIA	ROME, ITALY	TOKYO, JAPAN	MEXICO CITY, MEXICO	MUNICH, WEST GERMANY	MONTREAL, QUEBEC	MOSCOW, SOVIET UNION	LOS ANGELES, CALIFORNIA	SEOUL, SOUTH KOREA	BARCELONA, SPAIN	ATLANTA, GEORGIA	SYDNEY, AUSTRALIA	ATHENS, GREECE	BEIJING, CHINA	LONDON, ENGLAND
1896	1900	1904	1908	1912	1920	1924	1928	1932	1936	1948	1952	1956	1960	1964	1968	1972	1976	1980	1984	1988	1992	1996	2000	2004	2008	2012

MEDALS FOR THE AGES

DARA TORRES U.S. EVENTS: 50-METER FREESTYLE, 100-METER FREESTYLE, 100-METER BUTTERFLY, 4X100-METER FREESTYLE RELAY, 4X100-METER MEDLEY RELAY

OLYMPIC COMPETITIONS: 1984, 1988, 1992, 2000, 2008

In her athletic prime, American swimmer Dara Torres was a blur in the water as she raced her way to a total of nine medals in the Olympic Games of 1984, 1988, 1992, and 2000. And then, after it seemed that her day had passed, a supposedly "over-the-hill" Torres sneaked up on the world of women's swimming to snatch three more medals at the 2008 Olympics in Beijing and inspire any athlete thinking about a comeback, if not older folks on a grander scale.

Dara Torres (left) congratulates Britta Steffen after their thrilling race in 2008's 50-meter freestyle final

The 2008 Olympics were, in fact, Torres's third comeback. She had previously retired after the 1992 Olympics and skipped the Games of 1996, only to come back to compete in Sydney in 2000, winning two relay golds and a trio of bronze medals in individual events. After retiring a second time and bypassing the 2004 Games, Torres had her first child in 2006. To the surprise of many of her competitors, Torres un-retired again and began training for the 2008 Olympics. Not only did Torres qualify for the 2008 Games at the U.S. Olympic Trials in July 2008, she broke the American record in the 50-meter freestyle. On August 10, 2008, the 41-year-old became the oldest swimmer of either gender to garner a medal when she anchored the American 4x100-meter freestyle relay team that took silver. The medal was the fifth that Torres had earned in that relay event.

The ageless dynamo then took to the pool for the 50-meter freestyle. The event is swimming's equivalent of track's 100-meter dash—a flashy and explosive race, and one historically dominated by athletes with the fast, twitchy muscles of youth. Torres tore through the race in record American time again, finishing in 24.07 seconds. The time would have been a world record as well if it had not been for the mad dash of Britta Steffen of Germany, who clipped Torres to set the world record at 24.06 seconds. Mere minutes later, Torres joined in the American 4x100-meter medley relay team that netted her a third silver medal at the 2008 Games.

Torres's coach, Michael Lohberg, was hospitalized with a serious bone marrow disorder called aplastic anemia before the Beijing Games, thus leaving Torres to basically coach herself—another credit to her feats. "I think this performance ranks up there with the biggest performances in sports ever," said Lohberg, who watched her races from a hospital bed. "It puts Dara in the ranks of Michael Phelps, [basketball legend] Michael Jordan, [and golfing great] Tiger Woods. What she has done is really not measurable." Kara Lynn Joyce, an American swimmer who raced against Torres in the 50-meter freestyle and teamed with Torres in helping the American women win silver in the 4x100-meter freestyle and medley relays, was inspired by Torres's defiance of Father Time. Said Joyce, who was 22 years old in Beijing, "It gives me hope for another 20 years."

ATHENS, GREECE	PARIS, FRANCE	ST. LOUIS, MISSOURI	LONDON, ENGLAND	STOCKHOLM, SWEDEN	ANTWERP, BELGIUM	PARIS, FRANCE	AMSTERDAM, NETHERLANDS	LOS ANGELES, CALIFORNIA	BERLIN, GERMANY	LONDON, ENGLAND	HELSINKI, FINLAND	MELBOURNE, AUSTRALIA	ROME, ITALY	TOKYO, JAPAN	MEXICO CITY, MEXICO	MUNICH, WEST GERMANY	MONTREAL, QUEBEC	MOSCOW, SOVIET UNION	LOS ANGELES, CALIFORNIA	SEOUL, SOUTH KOREA	BARCELONA, SPAIN	ATLANTA, GEORGIA	SYDNEY, AUSTRALIA	ATHENS, GREECE	BEIJING, CHINA	**LONDON, ENGLAND**
1896	1900	1904	1908	1912	1920	1924	1928	1932	1936	1948	1952	1956	1960	1964	1968	1972	1976	1980	1984	1988	1992	1996	2000	2004	2008	**2012**

THE GAMES OF 2012

The 2012 Olympics were to be held in London, England. Londoners got the news in July 2005, and as is the case any time an Olympic host is selected, city and national officials sprang into action. Although seven years may seem to be plenty of time for preparation, it is in fact a small window when one considers that host cities typically need to create housing for thousands of

In 2012, London was to play host to its third Summer Olympiad, having done so in 1908 and 1948

international athletes and coaches (generally in a consolidated area known as the "Athletes' Village"), expand public transportation options (such as trains and buses), and build outdoor playing fields, indoor arenas, and other venues with enough seating—and grandeur—to be worthy of Olympic competition.

The numbers involved in the 2012 Games indicate just how large a venture it is to host an Olympiad. Some 10,500 athletes from 200 countries were to compete in London, with 2,100 medals awarded. About 8 million tickets were expected to be sold for the Games. And before any athletes arrived or any medals were awarded, it was anticipated that the total cost of London's Olympics-related building projects and other preparations would approach $15 billion.

Among those construction projects was the creation of Olympic Park, a sprawling gathering area in east London that was to function as a center of activity during the Games. From the park, people would be able to move to numerous athletic facilities in and around the city. Those facilities included the 80,000-seat Olympic Stadium, which was built to host track and field events as well as the opening and closing ceremonies; the new Basketball Arena, a temporary structure that was to be dismantled after the Games; and the $442-million Aquatics Centre, which was designed both to host swimming events and to serve as a kind of visitors' gateway to Olympic Park. Other notable venues included the North Greenwich Arena (which was to host gymnastics), the ExCeL center (boxing), Earls Court (indoor volleyball), and Horse Guards Parade (beach volleyball).

In July 2011, British prime minister David Cameron and IOC president Jacques Rogge reviewed all preparations and proudly declared that the city was nearly ready to welcome the world. "This has the makings of a great British success story," Cameron announced. "With a year to go, it's on time, it's on budget…. We must offer the greatest ever Games in the world's greatest country."

Rogge kicked off the one-year countdown to the Games by formally inviting countries around the world to send their greatest athletes to the British capital in 2012. "The athletes will be ready," said Rogge. "And so will London."

amateur — not a professional

Amateur Athletic Union (AAU) — a U.S. sports organization formed in 1888 that oversees and promotes amateur sports and physical fitness

anchor — in a relay event, the last (fourth) swimmer or runner to compete; the role often goes to a team's fastest overall athlete

asthma — a condition of the lungs that can cause wheezing and coughing and makes it difficult for a person to breathe

backstroke — a swimming stroke swum in an upward-facing position in which the arms move in an alternating, windmilling motion, while the legs and feet perform a flutter kick; it is also called the back crawl

bureaucratic — describing an administrative style characterized by excessive routine

butterfly — a swimming stroke swum in a downward-facing position in which both arms move in sync in an overhead motion, while the legs and feet perform a dolphin kick

communism — a form of government that has tight control over a country's resources and people; many communist countries were rivals of the U.S. from the late 1940s to the early 1990s

crawl stroke — a swimming stroke swum in a downward-facing position in which the arms move in an alternating, windmilling motion, while the legs and feet perform a flutter kick

cricket — a bat-and-ball game similar to baseball; it originated in England in the 1500s and is especially popular in England, India, and Australia

deck — the elevated, dry surface immediately next to a swimming pool

developing nations — the poorest countries of the world, which are generally characterized by a lack of health care and industry; most developing nations are in Africa, Asia, and Latin America

flip turn — a swimming maneuver done when swimmers reach one end of the pool, flip over underwater, and push off from the wall to quickly reverse direction

freestyle — describing a race in which any swimming stroke may be used; the crawl stroke is most often used, as it is generally regarded as the fastest swimming stroke

haphazard — disorganized and characterized by a lack of planning

heat — in swimming and other racing sports, one of multiple preliminary races used to determine the field for the final medal competition, which may be called the final heat

legs — the sections of a team relay race; in a swimming relay, one swimmer dives into the water as soon as the preceding swimmer touches the wall

medley — in swimming, a race that features a combination of four different swimming strokes, including butterfly, backstroke, breaststroke, and freestyle; such races can be swum individually or as a team relay

netball — a game similar to basketball that is played outdoors with a soccer ball; it originated in England in the late 1800s and is especially popular in England and Australia

prelims — in swimming and other racing sports, the races preceding the finals that serve to narrow the field to only the best competitors; the word is short for "preliminaries"

starter's mark — a sound, such as a horn or electronic tone, that signals the start of a swimming race

steroid — a chemical substance or drug that affects muscle growth; some athletes have used steroids illegally to become stronger and faster

undulating — moving with a smooth, wavelike motion

Selected Bibliography

Anderson, Dave. *The Story of the Olympics*. New York: HarperCollins, 2000.

Biondi, Matt. "Diary of a Champion." *Sports Illustrated*, October 3, 1988.

Guttmann, Allen. *The Olympics: A History of the Modern Games*. Urbana: University of Illinois Press, 2002.

Macy, Sue, and Bob Costas. *Swifter, Higher, Stronger: A Photographic History of the Summer Olympics*. Washington, D.C.: National Geographic, 2008.

Maraniss, David. *Rome 1960: The Olympics That Changed the World*. New York: Simon & Schuster, 2008.

Montville, Leigh. "Fast Lanes." *Sports Illustrated*, September 25, 2000.

Osborne, Mary Pope. *Ancient Greece and the Olympics*. New York: Random House, 2004.

Walters, Guy. *Berlin Games: How the Nazis Stole the Olympic Dream*. New York: William Morrow, 2006.

Web Sites

International Olympic Committee
www.olympic.org
This site is the official online home of the Olympics and features profiles of athletes, overviews of every sport, coverage of preparation for the 2012 Summer Games, and more.

Sports-Reference / Olympic Sports
www.sports-reference.com/olympics
This site is a comprehensive database for Olympic sports and features complete facts and statistics from all Olympic Games, including medal counts, Olympic records, and more.

INDEX

Published by Creative Education
P.O. Box 227, Mankato, Minnesota 56002
Creative Education is an imprint of
The Creative Company
www.thecreativecompany.us

Design and production by The Design Lab
Art direction by Rita Marshall

Printed by Corporate Graphics in
the United States of America

Photographs by Alamy (Daily Mail/Rex, Everett
Collection Inc), American Numismatic Society,
Dreamstime (Alain Lacroix, Studio 37), Getty
Images (AFP/AFP, Al Bello /Allsport, Simon Bruty/
Allsport, Simon Bruty /Sports Illustrated, MARTIN
BUREAU/AFP, Tony Duffy/Allsport, Focus on
Sport, Getty Images, Keystone, Keystone-France/
Gamma-Keystone, Heinz Kluetmeier /Sports
Illustrated, David Madison, Donald Miralle,
Popperfoto, Mike Powell /Allsport, Adam Pretty,
STAFF/AFP, Billy Stickland/ALLSPORT, FRANCOIS
XAVIER MARIT/AFP), Shutterstock (Antonio
Abrignani, Igor Golovniov, nadi555)

Library of Congress
Cataloging-in-Publication Data
LeBoutillier, Nate.
Swimming / by Nate LeBoutillier.
p. cm. — (Summer Olympic legends)
Includes bibliographical references and index.
Summary: A survey of the highlights and
legendary athletes—such as American Michael
Phelps—of the Olympic sport of swimming,
which has been part of the modern Summer
Games since 1896.
ISBN 978-1-60818-211-4
1. Swimmers—Biography—Juvenile literature.
2. Swimming—Juvenile literature. 3. Olympics—
Juvenile literature. I. Title.
GV837.9.L44 2012
796.210922 [B]—dc23   2011032497

CPSIA: 030111 PO1452

First Edition
9 8 7 6 5 4 3 2 1